This is
NEW ZEALAND

This is
NEW ZEALAND

Photographs Martin Barriball
Text Mervyn Dykes

REED

First published 1982 as *New Zealand's North Island in Colour*
and *New Zealand's South Island in Colour*
This edition first published 1992

Published by Reed Books, a division of Reed Publishing
Group (NZ) Ltd, 39 Rawene Road, Birkenhead, Auckland.
Associated companies, branches and representatives
throughout the world.

ISBN 0 7900 0275 2
© 1992 Reed Publishing (NZ) Ltd

Reprinted 1993

Printed in Hong Kong

Cover photograph of Lake Matheson by Noel Bartley

NORTH ISLAND

When the pioneers first encountered New Zealand's temperate climate, magnificent scenery and fertile soils they pronounced it "God's own country" — a land of wonders where crops and children grow with equal vigour; a land where steam and boiling mud and water burst from the ground and soaring glaciers made icy stairways to the sky; a land of opportunities for people prepared to work hard. New Zealand offered a new start; it was the new place to be.

People shaped this land to their needs with fire and steel; they gouged hills, erected concrete towers and slashing motorways. But for all that, their hold remained tenuous and the energy of their environment was such that nature could roll over their works in a few generations.

Men of legend tried to leave their marks in much the same way as more recent settlers. Maui, a legendary Maori hero, is said to have fished the North Island of New Zealand from the sea. His canoe was the older and more geologically stable South Island.

When they realised what lay before them, Maui's brothers raced on to Te Ika a Maui — The Fish of Maui — and hacked and carved out choice pieces for themselves.

The figures have passed into legend now, but the land remains: the larger South Island with its mountains, lakes, glaciers and wide-reaching plains; and the more populous North Island with its rolling green hills dotted with sheep and cattle, volcanoes, awesome thermal regions, bush-covered mountains and golden beaches.

From Cape Reinga at its northern tip to the capital city of Wellington in the south, New Zealand's North Island is a traveller's delight. The land holds an infinite variety of expressions and experiences. The people have dispositions as warm and inviting as the beaches of the Hibiscus Coast.

Some visitors race through the North Island on clockwork tours designed to cram as much as possible into the smallest capsule of time. Others go about their explorations at a more leisurely pace, stepping off well-worn tracks in search of the essence of the land and its people. But both groups will leave part of their hearts here and take something of New Zealand with them wherever they go.

This has always been so. The first explorers to visit New Zealand travelled half-way round the world to get here, spending months at sea in open canoes or sailing ships. Often they risked their lives in the process. They expected to find something different when they arrived, and they were not disappointed.

Some hundreds of years later that difference is still apparent, thanks to the strange timelessness of the Pacific. There is something hauntingly familiar about the country that will tease the deepest levels of memory. Is this North Island experience the way things were meant to be, with people and nature not too far removed?

We invite you to make your own voyage of discovery, either in person or through the pages of this book. We welcome you, but we warn you — you will never be the same again.

1. The Bay of Islands from the air.

1

1. The rocky outcrop of Cape Reinga on the northernmost part of the North Island juts into the meeting-place of the Tasman Sea and the Pacific Ocean. It has special significance to the Maori people. Legend has it that from this point the spirits of the Maori dead part company with New Zealand and begin the long journey to their ancestral homeland of Hawaiki. But whatever one's race or personality, the atmosphere and sense of timelessness at Cape Reinga mark it as a special place for all who answer its call.

2. By their nature, lighthouses are usually found in lonely places. Erected as beacons to guide ocean travellers through troubled waters, they dot the headlands and harbour entrances around New Zealand's rugged coastline. The sentinel at Cape Reinga, however, has a unique distinction. Although it could lay claim to being the most remote, it probably receives more visitors than all the other lighthouses in New Zealand put together. Each year thousands of people trek to it so they can say they have touched one of New Zealand's boundaries.

3. Cape Maria van Diemen, looking back towards Motuopao Island. The cape was named by explorer Abel Janszoon Tasman who discovered New Zealand in 1642.

2

3

1. Part of the history of Northland and its people is preserved in what has become one of the premier tourist attractions in the area, the Wagener Museum at Houhora. The collection includes Maori artefacts, kauri gum, natural history exhibits, relics from early whaling ships and Victoriana.

1

2. The North Island is rich in beautiful harbours, but the attractiveness of Whangaroa, on the east coast north of the Bay of Islands, belies its bloody history. From here, Hori, chief of the local Maoris, led his warriors in a raid on the Wesleyan Mission at Kaeo, and it was here, too, that the notorious "*Boyd* massacre" took place. The *Boyd* was a timber ship which called at Whangaroa to take on kauri logs for Australia. In revenge for the captain's flogging of a chief's son, local Maori people guided a shore party to a place where they said some kauri could be found. They murdered the men and at dusk returned to the *Boyd* dressed in the victims' clothes. Once aboard, the Maoris spared only a woman and two children. The *Boyd* itself came to a savage end when a spark from a Maori pipe fell into gunpowder. Today Whangaroa is world renowned as a big-game fishing port and a place of peace and beauty.

3. Tane, the Maori god of the forest, still has some huge attendants in the Waipoua State Forest. One of them is the giant kauri known as Te Matua Ngahere, or the Father of the Forest, with a girth of about 17 metres. During pioneer days the kauri was much sought after for masts and spars. Its clean, hard timber also excelled for use in buildings that were meant to last. Once huge forests of these giants extended over much of the Northland peninsula. Now the few that remain are protected by law. It will be a long time before the forests return — if ever. After 500 years a kauri is still little more than an adolescent. Elsewhere in the Waipoua State Forest is Tane Mahuta, reputed to be more than 1,200 years old. The names given to these trees show the reverence in which they were held by the Maori — a reverence now shared somewhat belatedly by the Pakeha, their European countrymen.

2

1

1.The friendship between humans and dolphins is well chronicled back to the time of the ancient Greeks. However, in the summer of 1955-6 a touch of magic came to the beach resort town of Opononi near the entrance to Northland's Hokianga Harbour. Children playing in the surf were joined suddenly by a dolphin, which quickly struck up an amazing friendship. Opo, as she became known, proved a tireless playmate. She allowed children to ride on her back, played ball and tag with them, performed for movie and still cameras and generally brought with her a spirit of fun that captured the hearts of New Zealanders everywhere. Her death at the end of that glorious summer was an event of such sadness that a statue was erected to preserve her memory and to pay tribute to the gifts of friendliness she brought.

2. Further up the Hokianga is Rawene, a quaint old timber town. This view of the harbour was taken in that vicinity.

2

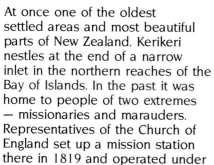

At once one of the oldest settled areas and most beautiful parts of New Zealand, Kerikeri nestles at the end of a narrow inlet in the northern reaches of the Bay of Islands. In the past it was home to people of two extremes — missionaries and marauders. Representatives of the Church of England set up a mission station there in 1819 and operated under the protection of the Ngai Tahu chief Hongi Hika. This same chieftain was the first in New Zealand to arm his warriors with muskets and in so doing was able to achieve a military supremacy over virtually all of the North Island tribes.

Today the name Kerikeri is synonymous with fruit and arts and crafts. Its orchards provide much of the country's citrus fruit, and in these pleasant surroundings, potters, artists and craftspeople of many persuasions have made their homes. However, reminders of the past are plentiful. Chief among them are the Stone Store at the Kerikeri Basin, now a museum, and the Kemp homestead, the oldest surviving building in New Zealand.

1. When the missionaries came to Kerikeri in the early 1800s, they built to last, whether it was in the spreading of the gospel or in the erection of more earthly signs of God's presence. A few metres from the historic Stone Store is a building commonly bracketed with it in tourist brochures — gracious Kemp House. Although it was built by the Reverend John Butler in 1822, Kemp House takes its name from a blacksmith and lay preacher, James Kemp, who occupied it 10 years later. Mr Kemp was one of the original mission workers and his descendants continued to live there until modern times. There are many unique features in the house's construction, and a tour is a rewarding experience.

2. If it is true that artists need peace and quiet to do their best work, it is hard to imagine a setting more inspiring than Kerikeri. There is a feeling of being close to nature and of energies more lasting than the fleeting sensations of the outside world. Potters, artists, spinners, weavers, workers in wood, leather and metal have been drawn to the district. Their roadside shops and studios tucked away in the bush attract a pilgrimage of art lovers who often have the advantage of being able to talk to the craftsmen and craftswomen at work.

3. Tales of sunken treasure have fired imaginations for centuries. For most people they remain tales, but at Paihia in the Bay of Islands there is the chance to see the real thing in a floating museum. Kelly Tarlton, one of New Zealand's best-known divers and treasure hunters, set up the museum to display the gold, jewellery and relics he has recovered from wrecks around the coast. Even the museum ship, the *Tui*, has an interesting past. Originally a trading scow, it has been rigged with spars from a barque wrecked on a Northland beach. Now it serves as a major tourist attraction without leaving its moorings.

1. Who today could imagine Russell township as "the hell-hole of the Pacific"? Yet that is what it was called when, in 1840 as Kororareka, a wild whaling town, it was the largest European settlement in New Zealand.

In order to escape its licentious image the name of Russell was later conferred on the township, after the country's first "capital" a short distance away. But this did not spell the end of riotous activity there. Hone Heke, nephew of the famous fighting chief Hongi Hika, felled the British flagpole no fewer than four times in protest at British presence in the area. Heke's men then attacked Russell, sparing only the churches and mission buildings from their torch. These days the bays and inlets, seen here swathed in early-morning mist, are given over to deep-sea fishing boats and the occasional cruise ship. And Russell township? It's better known as a holiday and tourist centre.

2. The American author Zane Grey renamed the Bay of Islands "The Angler's Eldorado" when, in a book of the same name, he extolled the virtues of the fishing. Grey, an enthusiastic salt-water and fresh-water fisherman, made several visits to the area in the late 1920s and early 1930s. The reputation he helped establish for the Bay of Islands as one of the world's best big-game fishing grounds remains to this day.

1

1. Here a striped marlin provides proof that the big fish are still biting in the Bay of Islands. In spite of the invasion by anglers from all over the world, records continue to be made. The skill and knowledge of the skippers and crews of the big-game boats is such that even a newcomer to the sport could end up with a trophy, a photograph and a tale or two to tell.

2. There is another kind of fish available at the Bay of Islands. Paihia carver, Joe Gamble, carves kauri reminders for unlucky fishermen and objects of art for those who appreciate the beauty of dolphins and fish.

3, 4. Fishing boats and pleasure craft at anchor near Russell.

2

3

4

1. Pompallier House, Russell, once part of the first Roman Catholic mission station in New Zealand.

2. A glimpse of Russell township from the hills behind.

3. This house on The Strand, Russell's picturesque waterfront, looks out over a peaceful bay in which whaling ships from around the world once lay at anchor.

1

2

3

1-3. A hui (Maori gathering) on the marae at Waitangi in the Bay of Islands.

4,5. Waitangi Day — part festival, part fun and part solemn commemoration. On 6 February 1840 Captain William Hobson of the Royal Navy and most of the paramount Maori chiefs of New Zealand signed the Treaty of Waitangi and founded a nation. Each year on 6 February this event is recalled in celebrations in front of the Treaty House, a beautiful old home where the original treaty was signed. Designed in the Georgian style, the house is open to visitors and annually thousands of New Zealanders and overseas tourists look through its rooms to sample a taste of history. Also of interest in the Treaty House grounds is the Maori Centennial Memorial meeting house or whare runanga. It is unique in that it contains carvings from many different tribes throughout the North Island instead of the usual set of carvings from a single tribe.

4

5

1

2

1. Travellers wait to board the ferry that will take them from Russell to Paihia. A variety of sightseeing cruises is available also, including the world famous "Cream Trip", a four-and-a-half hour cruise among the beautiful islands of the bay.

2. For those who like to see the sights at speed there's a faster alternative — a catamaran.

3. The catamaran lines up for its passage through the hole in the rock at Piercy Island, Cape Brett.

4. A view of the sights from the catamaran *Tiger Lily.*

1.2. One of the best features of the Bay of Islands is the large number of safe beaches which provide good swimming and easy launching for small boats.

3. Looking at the small wooden building that is Christ Church it is hard to believe that once hundreds of men swarmed around it locked in bloody combat. But a closer inspection provides proof in the form of bullet holes and the scars left by flying shot. The drama occurred when the Maori leader Hone Heke sacked the pioneer settlement of Kororareka, now Russell, putting to the torch all but the church and some associated buildings. Christ Church, built in 1836, is believed to be the oldest surviving church in New Zealand.

1. The principal centre of population in Northland is Whangarei city, situated on a beautiful natural harbour some 170 kilometres north of the metropolis of Auckland. Early records and Maori folklore indicate that it has always been a popular place to live. Safe anchorages, a river, forests, fertile soil, good fishing and a rugged screen of hills are only a few of the natural attractions Whangarei has to offer. The industrial life of the area is dominated by the Marsden Point oil refinery and oil-fired power station. Sheet-glass manufacturing and fertiliser and cement works are important, too, and counterbalance the attractions of Whangarei's congenial climate and proximity to the playgrounds of the "winterless" north.

2. Few cities can boast such an aquatic treasure as handy to suburban homes as the nearest supermarket. The Whangarei Falls are a delight whatever the season, and there is a choice of vantage points. The falls plunge into a narrow bush-covered ravine and are overlooked by a parking area at the top. The more adventurous can take easy bush paths to the foot of the falls for a closer view.

2

1

1

1.The towering Whangarei Heads which guard the entrance to Whangarei Harbour loom over the surrounding countryside providing a backdrop steeped in Maori legend. The drive from the city to the heads is a particularly rewarding one. The road winds through a series of small bays fringed with pohutukawa trees with flame-red blooms. Tiers of cottages are stacked along the hillsides. Several points offer excellent views of Marsden Point on the opposite side of the harbour, the bright-orange gas flare from the oil refinery acting as a beacon visible for many kilometres. Many of the bays offer safe swimming and boating.

2.What better place to go if you have time on your hands in Whangarei than the world-famous Clapham's Clock Museum? Named after a resident who began the collection, the museum includes a fascinating array of more than 400 timepieces from many parts of the world and several centuries. Children delight in the novelty clocks, but history buffs and lovers of beauty will be just as intrigued.

3. Muriwai Beach is beloved of surfers and fishermen throughout the north. Within easy reach of Auckland city, it is also a popular spot for picnics and family outings the year round. During summer, fishermen with long surf-casting poles try their luck for snapper and other ocean delicacies. The ocean is a wonderful playmate, but Muriwai should be treated with respect. Unwary fishermen have been swept from rocks and drowned. Swimmers are urged constantly to remember that the sea can be deadly and to swim within the areas covered by beach patrols.

2

3

1. Auckland is rich in beaches, and its North Shore particularly so. The notched eastern coastline offers a series of delightful bays almost at the front doors of the homes that press right to clifftop and water's edge. Browns Bay, in the foreground, retains its original village atmosphere, but has a major shopping centre screened from the beach by a thin line of trees and buildings. Mairangi Bay, four notches to the south, is similar. Even in bustling Takapuna city, just across the harbour bridge from downtown Auckland, the shoppers are less than five minutes from sand and surf. For a boat-loving, outdoors people the North Shore beaches are gems beyond price.

2. Mission Bay was once the scene of early missionary activity in Auckland. Today the district is one of Auckland's most desirable housing areas and comes complete with a lovely swimming beach and attractive fountain.

3. Just about everywhere one goes in Auckland, there is Rangitoto Island slotted snugly against the horizon. This symmetrical volcanic cone is the youngest of the islands in the Hauraki Gulf. Its name means "Bloody Sky" and is reminiscent of the titanic eruption that occurred when the island blasted itself out of the ocean little more than 700 years ago.

4. One of Auckland's best-known landmarks is One Tree Hill, here silhouetted against a darkening sky. The hill, like so many of the commanding sites around the city, was once a Maori pa and is now an extinct volcano. On the summit is the tomb of Sir John Logan Campbell, one of the founding fathers of Auckland. Reaching skyward with the tree that gives the hill its name is an obelisk erected as a tribute to the Maori people. Sir John's wooden cottage, built in 1843, is preserved as a museum at the foot of the hill in Cornwall Park.

5. An Auckland city sunset viewed from Okahu Bay.

2

3

4

5

1

1. After a hard week at the office what could be better than to hang from the trapeze of a sleek yacht as it cuts through the waters of the harbours and bays around Auckland? For those who like the sea, but do not have a boat of their own there are ferry and launch cruises around the Hauraki Gulf.

2. Love of the sea and sailing has reached epidemic proportions in Auckland. With ownership of a small yacht or power boat more popular than a second car, estimates of the size of the city's fleet of private pleasure craft range upwards from 50,000. Not only do some of the world's best sailors train on its waters but the city has also produced boat designers, sailmakers and boat builders of international ranking. The city has a choice of harbours to sail on and just beyond them lie the vivid blue waters of the island-studded Hauraki Gulf. Little wonder that the city's January anniversary-day regatta is the biggest in the world.

3. The yellow and black sails of a fleet of hire catamarans eager for flight offer a siren call to weekend sailors.

4. The marina at Auckland's Halfmoon Bay provides mooring and berthing facilities.

2

3

4

1.

1. Sunlight tips masts and sails
with gold in the Westhaven boat
harbour.

2. Auckland's trademark, so far
as works of people are concerned,
is its "coathanger" harbour bridge
linking the North Shore with the
city centre. It also serves as the
main route north from Auckland,
connecting at both ends of its
1,100-metre span with a
sophisticated motorway system.
When the bridge was built in 1965
sceptics said it would never be
used to capacity. However, its
original four traffic lanes soon had
to be doubled to eight, and it was
joined by a second bridge further
up the harbour. The developments
with the harbour bridge (seen here
looking towards the Westhaven
boat harbour and the city) are
symbolic of the rapid growth of
the city. Auckland began rather
shakily in 1840, enjoyed a brief
period as the nation's capital and
has since become New Zealand's
biggest population centre with
more than 760,000 people in its
urban areas.

2

1.The face of downtown Auckland changes steadily. What was once one of the busiest intersections — that of Queen and Quay Streets near the waterfront — is now closed off by Queen Elizabeth Square. Nearby are shopping malls, hotels and a huge conference centre. This pedestrian plaza, with its strange sculpture capturing the essence of wind and water, counter-balances the civic square further up Queen Street.

2. In Auckland's early days Parnell was one of the most desirable of the inner suburbs. But by the 1960s it was a run-down ghost of former glories. The city was faced with the choice whether to restore or destroy. It opted for restoration, and the result — a shopping centre unmatched in New Zealand — won a national tourist award. It is a must for those who like to shop amid the charms of another age.

3.Quay Street on the Auckland waterfront is one of the most easily recognised parts of the city. To the left is the fringe of the downtown commercial area, and to the right, the Waitemata Harbour. The historic ferry building on the right in the middle distance, a reminder of bygone ages, is dwarfed by the newcomers across the street.

1

2

3

1, 2.The very name smacks of something special. Karangahape Road — sheer music the way it rolls from the tongue. But so much of Polynesia is music, and as Auckland is the world's biggest Polynesian city its multi-cultural charms come together like the instruments in a symphony orchestra. Karangahape Road forms the crossbar to a "T" that it makes with Queen Street in the very heart of Auckland City. It is a place of bargains and shopping surprises, and everywhere there is evidence of the South Pacific.

3.Costumed dancers celebrate at a wine festival in the "grape belt" — Auckland's western suburbs. Most of the vineyards were planted by settlers from what is now Yugoslavia. There are strong Croatian communities in both Auckland and Wellington. Others settled further north where they hunted buried deposits of valuable kauri gum.

4. Auckland is home to the world's biggest "fun run", the annual Round the Bays event which has drawn fields of more than 50,000 people. At quieter times, though, there are still joggers everywhere, and if the fabled runner's high fails to appear there is always the joy of the surroundings to compensate, in this case Mission Bay.

5. Parnell Baths — a large complex of saltwater swimming facilities near the Tamaki waterfront.

4

5

1

2

1. In the uncertain times after fighting in the Bay of Islands in 1845, the citizens of Auckland lived with the fear of invasion by hostile Maori tribes. Governor Grey established five "pensioner villages", forming an outer defensive screen overlooking the main waterway approaches to the township. In return for light military duties , former soldiers from the Royal New Zealand Fencibles were granted cottages on one-acre plots of land. Some 700 military settlers arrived and soon began to till their land, their labours supplying Auckland and ships in port with fruit and fresh vegetables. It is appropriate, therefore, that this former Fencible cottage in Howick, Auckland, should now be a restaurant. Known as Bell House, it caters to modern generations who come to dine in the shadow of the past.

2.The fittings in the cottages were simple by modern standards, but quite comfortable for people establishing themselves in a new land. Modern decorators often strive to recapture the pioneer look — the charm is undeniable.

3. The Polynesian collection at the Auckland War Memorial Museum is one of the finest in the world. The entrance is commanded by an impressive Maori canoe and meeting house that show to good advantage the artistry of those who fashioned them. There is an atmosphere about the exhibits that prompts reflection. For those who choose to sit on seats outside the meeting house and watch the reactions of the passers-by, there is a chance for some education in Maoritanga, too. At the push of a button, a taped programme explaining the history of many of the carvings and constructions runs tirelessly through its cycle of information. And the pakeha? Part of their history is upstairs in the equally intriguing Pioneer Street.

4. An aerial view of the museum which is set in the parklands of Auckland Domain.

2

1. Children and steam trains are a fun-filled combination. The Glenbrook Express, which runs on a special track south of the city, is a museum on wheels. Steam train enthusiasts come from miles around to ride the rails, and it's a winner as a family outing.

2. Carriage interior.

3. Auckland's Museum of Transport and Technology on the Great North Road boasts a working tramway among its attractions

3

1, 2. The big question at all zoos is whether the people are there to look at the animals or vice versa. Over a fence or in every cage or compound, there is an animal looking back, be it quizzical emu or haughty camel. Auckland Zoo is the biggest and best in the country, and a determined attempt has been made to provide attractions for children once they have seen enough of animals. The zoo is situated in a bush reserve at Western Springs, near one of the most magnificent museums in the Southern Hemisphere — the Museum of Transport and Technology. Both are on bus routes from the city.

3. The emblem of the north, the pohutukawa tree, provides a brilliant sight when it is aflame with blossom. Pohutukawas grow in stately avenues and cling by the most precarious of toeholds to clifftops throughout the north and even on the islands of the Hauraki Gulf. Their blossoms are usually red, although there are rarer yellow and white varieties. Maori travellers sighting New Zealand for the first time are reputed to have said: "Throw away your red feather head-dress; there are many red plumes dancing on the shore." Long may they continue to dance.

4

5

4,5. Fertile lands to the south of Auckland city provide much of its food from huge market gardens. In this instance the harvest is nothing to cry about, although the field is full of the best Pukekohe onions. Just over the back is the Pukekohe raceway, home to the New Zealand Grand Prix and international stars of motor racing.

1. All along the Coromandel Peninsula there are places where fishermen can try their luck or people can go to commune with nature. This delightful bay is located near Thames, the principal township in the area located at the foot of the Coromandel Range at the south-west edge of the peninsula. In the past people dug gold from Coromandel's hills. Today, one of the biggest industries is a happy reversal of this process — tourists flock to Coromandel in their thousands, bringing "gold" back to the peninsula communities.

2. Excellent sea views can be had from the fertile farmlands of the Coromandel.

3. Fishing on the rising tide at Whitianga on the Coromandel Peninsula. The district can boast a history of settlement going back more than 1,000 years to Kupe, the fabled explorer ancestor of the Maoris who is thought to have discovered New Zealand for his people about 950A.D. "Whitianga" is a contraction of "Whitianga-a-Kupe", or "The Crossing Place of Kupe". English explorer, Captain James Cook, was

also familiar with the area, writing extensively in his journals of a place where the climate was gentle enough for people to sleep outdoors. The same qualities are appreciated today by people who have made it a favourite holiday spot.

2

3

1

2

3

1. Right in the heart of Hamilton is Lake Rotoroa (not to be confused with the similar-sounding Rotorua near the city of the same name). This lovely lake is artificial, but nature has accepted the assistance graciously and the area surrounding Hamilton Lake, as it is sometimes known, has become a playground. Yachts and rowing shells cut across the lake, and around its shores are picnic areas, a mini golf course, skating rink, swings, slides and everything else an adventurous child could wish for.

2. In the early days of New Zealand the Waikato River was navigable by ocean-going sailing vessels for many of its 425 kilometres. Now it has been dammed so often to provide hydro-electricity that much of it has silted up. However, it is still a thing of great beauty, this longest of New Zealand rivers, particularly where it flows through the booming provincial city of Hamilton. Actually, Hamilton has been booming since the late 1950s, but given the fertility of the surrounding countryside and the importance of the region to the country's agriculturally based economy, what could be more natural?

3. Rustling fields of maize abound on the fertile Hauraki Plains to the south of the Firth of Thames. Originally, much of the area was swampland, but drainage and skilled farming techniques have wrought dramatic changes.

1

2

3

4

1-3. The Waikato district is as rich in Maori history and culture as a chocolate cake is in calories. Nowhere is this more evident than at Ngaruawahia, home of Maori royalty and site of a thrilling annual regatta. Ngaruawahia is only a few minutes from Hamilton by car, and each March thousands of New Zealanders converge on the small township to enjoy the regatta and associated activities. They can see Maori war canoes glide by in the river, a sight Europeans might not have lived to describe little more than 100 years ago.
Then there is canoe hurdling, a combination of skill and fun. Canoes race up to and over log barriers set just above the surface of the water. For the unlucky this means a swim and for the conquerors a cheer from the crowds on the riverbanks. Waikato is also home to one of New Zealand's most famous rowing clubs, the members of which have excelled in regattas as far away as Europe and North America. They, too, have their place in the Ngaruawahia festival. And everywhere, for everything that is done, there is an appreciative audience — even if some do have transistor radios to keep in touch with the outside world.

4. Not just one cave, but many, the Waitomo Caves are one of the world's major tourist attractions. Besides the weird and wonderful limestone formations there are glow-worm grottos that recreate the spangled beauty of the night sky. Waitomo (the name applies to the district as well as the caves) is 75 kilometres west of Hamilton. Regular tours of the caves are available and there is hotel accommodation nearby for those who take their time with their explorations. The glow-worms are of a different type to those found elsewhere in the world, apart from some distant relatives in Australia. To visit their haunt is to step into a place of enchantment.

1

1. Ocean Beach at Mount **Maunganui**, enhanced by the glow of dawn. While "The Mount", as it is known affectionately by most New Zealanders, is only 250 metres high, it gives a commanding view of the surrounding countryside. This fact was appreciated by Maoris who built a fortress on the site.

2. **The Wairoa River near Tauranga** offers plenty of thrills for those who like their water white, wild and woolly.

2

1, 2. Sunrise gilds the masts in the Tauranga Boat Harbour. Tauranga and its sister settlement, Mount Maunganui, together comprise one of New Zealand's most popular holiday areas, with whole cities of campers moving in each summer to take advantage of the temperate climate, pleasant beaches and fishing opportunities.

3. Situated just north of East Cape, Whangaparaoa Beach must have been a welcome sight to the Maori occupants of the canoes *Arawa* and *Tainui* who are said to have made landfall there after the long journey from Hawaiki. Fresh water cascades down to the beach for an added bonus.

1

2

3

1, 2. The East Cape of the North Island receives the first sun of each new day and all the world's capitals have to wait their turn. It's well worth the pilgrimage for those who like to be at the head of the line.

3. Waihau Bay is one of many popular East Cape camping places in summer. Here, and at the numerous other fine beaches and bays accessible from the East Coast Road, holidaymakers may enjoy the exceptional climate and scenery in relative tranquility.

4. The stamp of Captain James Cook is firmly imprinted on Tolaga Bay. Many of the streets in the small East Coast township are named after Cook, his ships or their crews. This reinforced concrete wharf testifies to a past as a bustling commercial port.

4

1. Just a short walk away from Tolaga Bay is Cooks Cove where, in 1769 and 1779, the master navigator refilled his water casks at what is now known as Cooks Well.

2. The city of Gisborne lies on the shores of Poverty Bay on the East Cape, midway between Tolaga Bay and the Mahia Peninsula. It was the site of the first European landing on New Zealand soil and has blossomed into a primary produce centre and starting point for holidaymakers.

3, 4. Board riders are of a breed that will travel many miles for the right set of surf, and remoteness is no obstacle to their enjoyment. Indeed, there is much more than surfing to enjoy in the solitude and beauty of such places as Mahia Peninsula. The peninsula is a stubby spear of land that thrusts southward at the northern extremity of Hawke Bay. Like many parts of the east coast, it has a long history of human occupation — by New Zealand standards, anyway!

3

4

1, 2. Nearly 206,000 hectares of rugged bush country make up New Zealand's easternmost national park. The Urewera National Park also contains beautiful Waikaremoana, the lake of rippling waters. The district is popular for its fishing, scenery and hunting. The Mokau Inlet is on the northern shoreline.

3. The reddish hue of rata flowers stains the bush near Lake Waikaremoana.

1

2

1. The Mokau Falls tumble over a 30-metre cliff, providing a constant attraction for passing motorists. The Urewera National Park is riddled with rivers and streams and there are several fine falls that are reasonably accessible.

2. Kereru, the native wood pigeon, is never far from berry bushes. A large bird with streaks of green and purple in its plumage, it is a surprisingly graceful flier.

3. The Hawke's Bay Aquarium at Napier houses an impressive display of ocean and tropical fish and tuatara and other reptiles.

4, 5. If animals have personalities the key trait of seals and dolphins would have to be a sense of fun. Not only do the ocean mammals at Napier's Marineland delight thousands of children and adults each year but they have a whale of a time in the process.

4

5

When Captain James Cook
anchored off this point in 1769 a
group of local Maoris tried to
kidnap his Tahitian interpreter's
servant boy. More than 200 years
later this incident is recalled in the
name given to the cape, which has
earned fame for another reason —
its bird colony. Cape Kidnappers is
home to the only known mainland
gannetry in the world. It is possible
to hike to the sanctuary from the
township of Clifton seven
kilometres away, but many people
take the alternative "safari" by
four-wheel drive vehicle from the
city of Napier on the coast further
north. Cape Kidnappers is at the
southernmost part of Hawke Bay,
and part of the walking route from
Clifton is along the beach. The
gannets are the large white
Australasian variety.

1. If it can be grown, it's probably grown in Hawke's Bay. The district vies annually with Nelson and Blenheim for the title of sunshine capital of New Zealand, and its market gardens yield prodigious quantities of fruit and vegetables. Nothing is more symbolic of the good life than a harvest of grapes such as these at Havelock North.

2. For those who like their grapes in bottles, the Te Mata Vineyard keeps open house. Visitors are able to sample the wares in the wine cellar surrounded by vats of red, white and true.

3. Even in Rotorua, the heart of New Zealand's most active thermal region, there is peace and serenity. This idyllic setting for the ancient game of bowls is in the Government Gardens not more than a few minutes from the city's main shopping district. Bowls is one of the most popular games in the country — some would say the most popular, in spite of the more robust appeal of rugby football.

1

2

3

1

1, 2. The ancient Romans were famous for their love of hot baths and the best in plumbing and central heating. So, too, were the Rotorua Maoris, but there are two important differences. When the Maoris arrived at Whakarewarewa the systems were already installed and they are still functioning today. Warm water bubbles up from the ground at temperatures ideal for bathing. Close at hand are boiling pools where the lady of the whare (house) can still cook food by dangling it in the water in a flax basket. Elsewhere in the city many homes are heated with the steam that squirts from rocks and fissures everywhere.

3. "Tread carefully all who come this way", could well be the warning from this carved figure at the entrance to a model Maori pa

near the Whakarewarewa thermal area, Rotorua. Although flimsy by the standards of the past, the pallisades give tourists an idea of the way things were when taniwhas lurked in the waterways and visitors who came calling might want more than a room for the night.

2

3

1

2

1, 2. However, when it comes to Pohutu Geyser only the foolhardy would want to get too close. There are seats set back a respectful distance for those who wish to wait for the geyser to blow its top. This it does several times a day, sending steam and water fountaining as high as 32 metres and often playing for more than half an hour.

3. At Wairakei, a few kilometres north of Taupo, huge clouds of steam billowing across the highway can make it look as if the earth has cracked open and an eruption is in progress. The noise and trembling ground seem to confirm this diagnosis. But relax, everything is under control. This is the site of the Wairakei Geothermal Power Station, which harnesses the energy of steam bores to produce electricity.

4,5. Between Wairakei and Rotorua lies the impressive Waimangu thermal district, which includes a large boiling lake known as the Cauldron.

3

4

5

1, 2. Some are bigger, higher, or prettier, but for sheer rock-trembling presence the Huka Falls are unmatched in New Zealand. Five kilometres north of Lake Taupo, the Waikato River is compressed suddenly into a 15-metre-wide rocky cleft about 230 metres long. At the same time the river bed falls eight metres as the torrent growls and jostles its way free of such impertinence. Finally, the seething mass of creamy blue-green foam spouts over the 11-metre drop of the falls proper and hammers into a deep bowl that has been scoured out over the ages. The water slowly loses its vivid colours as the river regains its composure and more realistic boundaries. The timid can view the spectacle from a loop road off the main highway. Those who are bolder can try a narrow bridge that spans the very brink of the falls.

3

3, 4. There is an old story about a tourist who arrived at his Taupo hotel in the dead of night and awoke the next morning thinking he was by the sea. This is an easy mistake to make because Lake Taupo, which extends over 619 square kilometres and is 160 metres deep, displays many of the moods of the ocean.

Taupo is an important holiday and recreation centre with a world-wide reputation for the quantity and quality of its rainbow and brown trout. For fishermen Taupo is the place to be, whether trolling from a boat off the mouth of the Tauranga-Taupo River, or as a "paling" in the celebrated "picket fence" where the Waitahanui River enters the lake.

4

1

2

1-6. With all that water around
there is plenty of opportunity
to indulge in aquatic pursuits
of all kinds, or simply to
relax around the lakeshore. The
rivers and streams associated with
Lake Taupo widen the scope of
activities further, and canoeists are
welcome on the Tongariro River —
so long as they don't scare the fish!

3

4

5

6

1-3. Motorists on the main
north-south highway always keep a
lookout for the symmetrical cone
of Mount Ngauruhoe (2,291 metres).
They usually have plenty to see as
Ngauruhoe grumbles and fumes
away to preserve its reputation as
the most continuously active of
New Zealand's volcanoes. It is one
of three major peaks in the
Tongariro National Park on the
central volcanic plateau to the
south of Lake Taupo. While
scientists clamber over the cone
and even peer down its awful
throat, they do so with a healthy
respect. Tourists are left to admire
the mountain from a distance or
bestow their favours on Mount
Tongariro (1,968 metres), 3
kilometres away to the north, or
the twin-peaked Mount Ruapehu
(2,797 metres), 16 kilometres to
the south. A good place for
admiring Ngauruhoe is from the
vicinity of the Mahuia Rapids.

1

1, 2.Mount Ruapehu is the highest peak in the North Island and gets the lion's share of attention from tourists. It has fully developed ski-fields on several of its slopes and even boasts a hot crater lake surrounded by snow.

3. Here students at the Turoa ski school learn what fun is all about.

1

2

3

1-3. Tongariro National Park was gifted to the nation by the Maori chief Te Heuheu Tukino IV (Horonuku) and other leaders of the Tuwharetoa tribe in 1887. They wished the sacred mountains to remain protected by their girdles of surrounding land for all time. There are many fine walks throughout the park, including that to the picturesque Tawhia Falls near The Chateau. Among the distinctive flora of the park is the umbrella fern and the native clematis.

4. Sheep graze on farmlands at the foot of Mount Ruapehu.

5. The Queen Elizabeth II Army Memorial Museum at Waiouru houses firearms, artillery, medals, insignia and uniforms used during military campaigns from the Maori Land Wars to Vietnam.

1

1. When it comes to superlatives, Mount Egmont is deserving. They all fit this central jewel in the Egmont National Park. An almost perfect volcanic cone rising abruptly from rich, green farmland is a sight that cries out to be photographed. The 2,518-metre peak has even been compared with Japan's Fujiyama, although the observer has to avoid the blemish of Fantham's Peak, an alternative crater bulging out of the southern slopes. Like Fujiyama, Egmont stands in splendid isolation. According to Maori legend he was chased there by the mountains of the central plateau when he paid too much attention to the charms of Tongariro's wife.

2. Taranaki, long famous for its pastures, is now rapidly becoming New Zealand's energy centre thanks to strikes of oil and natural gas. But whatever happens, Egmont will still be there to keep a watch over such modern-day attention grabbers as the Kapuni natural gas field and its flares.

3. In Maori mythology the legendary hero Maui hauled the North Island from the sea. Today the Maui natural gas platform, 34 kilometres off the Taranaki coast, produces new treasures. The gas is piped ashore to the Oaonui treatment station where it is prepared for its various roles. The gas reserves are expected to last beyond the year 2000, but with intense interest in exploration both offshore and onshore there is always the hope that there's more where that came from.

2

3

1

2

3

4

5

1. Ever since they were discovered in 1883, people have been coming to admire the Dawson Falls in Egmont National Park. Once they are there, a whole range of alternative activities opens up. Dawson Falls is now a resort area and one of the favoured starting points for climbers wishing to scale Mount Egmont. The falls are 18 metres high and were named after their discoverer, a postmaster named Thomas Dawson.

2. The Rangitikei River passes through some of the most rugged areas of the central North Island on its way to the sea south of Wanganui. The main highway between Auckland and Wellington carves its way through the hills nearby, as does the main trunk railway line, its course made easier by huge deviations and viaducts near Mangaweka. The river valley opens out into cliff-lined plains that are productive farmlands. The effect is wild and wonderful.

3. In rugged country waterfalls abound.

4. The Raukawa Falls are on the Mangawhero River, which rushes from Tongariro National Park to join the Whangaehu River north-east of Wanganui.

5. A tunnel of trees brings a touch of summer peace to the Parapara Road between Wanganui and Raetihi. This route follows the Mangawhero River for much of its course.

Rich in Maori history and as long on beauty as it is in kilometres, the Wanganui River is second in importance only to the Waikato in the North Island. Legends have it that the riverbed was carved out by Taranaki (the Maori name for Mount Egmont) as he fled the jealous Tongariro.

In the early days, the Wanganui was an important canoe route for travelling Maoris. Later, European settlers used a steamer service and today tourists still enjoy visiting the Wanganui's wilder places by leisurely launch, speedy jet boat or canoe. Bush-lined gorges on the upper reaches increase its air of mystery, but make voyages of discovery especially rewarding.

The township of Wanganui at the rivermouth dates back to 1840, the year of the signing of the Treaty of Waitangi. But there had been Maori settlers there for centuries. Today the "river city" is the centre of a thriving agricultural region to which come wool buyers representing clients from as far away as Europe. There are many pleasant drives in and around its environs.

1, 2. Students from many nations pass through this avenue of trees each year on their way to the Massey University campus at Palmerston North. Hailed as the most beautiful university in New Zealand, it specialises in agricultural sciences and often hosts international conventions and seminars.

3. Distinctive haystacks dot the farmland around the Rangitikei township of Bulls, midway between the cities of Palmerston North and Wanganui. The town's name comes from an English settler named James Bull who ran a hotel and store there. Bull, a noted carver, has examples of his work among the panelling in the House of Commons, half a world away in London.

4

4. The small Manawatu town of Feilding has an importance beyond its size. It is a service centre for surrounding farms which produce sheep, cattle and mixed crops. The big day of the week is sale day when the auctioneer is king and farmers come to buy, sell or just keep an eye on things. Less than 20 kilometres away is the major provincial centre, Palmerston North.

5. Sheep outnumber humans by nearly 23 to one in New Zealand. So far as the nation's economy is concerned, their fleece really is golden. About 75 per cent of New Zealand's export income is earned by agricultural products, and the farming expertise behind it is respected the world over. New Zealand is ranked among the top three trading nations in the world for meat, wool and dairy products. So what could be more typical than the sight of grazing sheep on a Manawatu farm?

5

1

2

1. New Zealand's 1,600 kilometres of often wild coastline took a heavy toll of early shipping. Part of the answer was a network of lighthouses established to save lives and assure the goods got to market. The Castlepoint Lighthouse on the Wairarapa coast still guards what for the pioneers was an important port, but the railways have taken its business away. Castlepoint continues to remind passing shipping of one thing that hasn't changed — the long fingers of rock that reach out to clutch the unwary.

2. The sloshing of surf and pounding hooves make a magical combination. Horse racing is one of the most popular New Zealand pastimes, and while racegoers have their Trenthams and Epsoms, beach meetings, such as this one at Castlepoint in the Wairarapa, have a special appeal.

3. Farmlands near Greytown were once part of an isolated rural community separated from Wellington by the Rimutaka Ranges. Now the railway lines punch through the hills — one of the tunnels being nine kilometres long — and a highway winds over the top. The Wairarapa farmlands still have their own identity, but Greytown, the oldest settlement in the area, is now only 80 kilometres from Wellington by road and doubles as a weekend retreat and even as a commuter base.

3

1

2

3

4

1, 2. The flaring fenders of a Bugatti a long way from home are one of many attractions at the Southward Museum, which houses some of the world's rarest cars. The museum is just north of Paraparaumu, an easy hour's drive from Wellington.

3. Silver-grey tiers of sand, surf and sky blend together as a solitary walker enjoys the serenity of a west coast beach near Wellington.

4. Who says beaches have to be sandy? The Makara Walkway, which skirts the edge of a rocky bay near Wellington city, demonstrates a charm of its own. There is good fishing in this vicinity.

2

1. Wellington harbour from Mount Victoria.

2. Named after its discoverer, Captain James Cook, the strait separating the North and South Islands of New Zealand contains some of the roughest ocean in the world. It is situated in the notorious "Roaring Forties" wind belt, and matters are complicated further by high land masses acting as a funnel for the gales. In spite of this the strait has many peaceful days and is a favourite testing ground for long distance swimmers. Inter-island ferries are popular both for strait crossings and day excursions. However, Barretts Reef on the western side of the entrance to Wellington Harbour was the site of the wrecking of the ferry *Wahine* in a storm in April 1968.

3. Putting best whiskers forward for the camera, a sea lion lolls among the curious onlookers at Red Rocks, south of the Wellington suburb of Island Bay. A few minutes further south at Sinclair Head there is a seal colony.

3

4. Parades of surf lifesavers are a common sight on the beaches in New Zealand and Australia. Surf clubs provide crack rescue teams, who polish their skills between rescues at surf carnivals and contests.

5. Beaches are focal points for animal and human activity in New Zealand. A line of red-beaked gulls waits patiently on a wall at Oriental Bay in downtown Wellington for crusts scattered by lunchtime sunbathers.

6. Even within the confines of Wellington Harbour there are many popular swimming and picnic spots. Scorching Bay is one of a series of pleasant notches along the eastern side of the Miramar Peninsula.

4

5

6

2

1. A typical Wellington scene — surburban homes stacked high on hillsides overlooking the Evans Bay boat harbour. With land at a premium in the capital city, every available home-site is used.

2. The main north-south highway merges with the Wellington Motorway and thrusts to the very feet of high-rise buildings in The Terrace, the home of big business in the capital.

3. Residential homes clinging to bush-clad slopes form the backdrop to this scene of Wellington's container shipping terminal.

3

1

2

3

1. Few visitors to Wellington leave without taking at least one ride on the cable car. The route climbs from the shops of Lambton Quay past Kelburn Park and Victoria University to the suburb of Kelburn. The park offers fine views of the harbour, and the final stop is near the famous Botanical Gardens.

2. Designed by the eminent British architect Sir Basil Spence, the additions to Parliament Buildings represent the centre of political power in New Zealand. Known as "The Beehive", the tower is linked to the older buildings in the complex which were modelled on the British Parliament at Westminster. In spite of its unusual

4

design, The Beehive won speedy acceptance and fitted easily into the Wellington scene.

3,4. Dawn casts a golden glow over the city's commercial centre.

1

2

3

4

1. The other major centre of power in New Zealand is the game of rugby, in which leviathan forward packs churn through mud in pursuit of the elusive ball. No one is very certain whether rugby is a game or a religion here, but anyone can tell you that New Zealanders are world champions at it.

2. A colourful crowd of sports fans at Wellington's Athletic Park.

3. Members of the New Zealand Symphony Orchestra.

4. The amusement attractions at the Wellington Trade Fair provide fun for people of all ages.

Sunrise over Lyall Bay, Wellington.

SOUTH ISLAND

Entering Milford Sound

Maui, the Maori hero of legend, is said to have hauled the North Island of New Zealand from the sea. For this purpose he needed a sturdy canoe, which he found in the larger and geologically older South Island. By all systems of measurement it is a most remarkable vessel.

The South Island, and Stewart Island at its foot, together cover some 15,150 hectares — not a large area by world standards, but embracing an incredible variety of scenery, some with a beauty that defies description.

Easily the most striking feature is the serrated mountain spine, the Southern Alps, which divides the island into two longitudinally. However, there are other distinct regions that make equally important separate contributions to the marvellous whole: in the north are the sunshine-rich market gardens and beaches of Nelson and Marlborough; down the eastern side of the alps run the fertile alluvial Canterbury Plains; and across the divide is the raw, craggy West Coast, which is still a frontier today. The south-west of the South Island is known as Fiordland. Words cannot describe adequately its incredible beauty, which seems to have the power to touch hearts and change lives. And to the south-east lie the twin provinces of Otago and Southland.

From 1861 men flocked to Otago from all over the world in search of gold. They were hard, hopeful men, some fired by greed but others wanting no more than the chance of a new life in a new land. Into this second category fell the settlers, many of whom came to New Zealand in large groups as part of regional colonisation programmes. They made the most lasting contributions of all who came. Whereas the miners took what they wanted and left, the settlers were soon engaged in a longer struggle against daunting odds.

Patterns emerged in settlement, too. Christchurch today retains its strong English influence, with evidence of a few Scottish threads running through. At Akaroa on Banks Peninsula there is a pocket of French influence, which residents are proud to maintain. Dunedin in the deep south is staunchly Scottish and boasts its own six-metre statue of Robbie Burns.

The South Island set much of the early pace for development in New Zealand. Rich gold finds fuelled industrial development in Dunedin to the extent that, for many years, it was the country's leading manufacturing and commercial centre. Here also New Zealand's first university was established, and Dunedin's rich brought in treasures from many parts of the world to grace their homes.

Today the South Island is a victim of a population drift to the north. In 1992 about 70 per cent of New Zealand's population lives in the North Island, with the biggest concentration centred on Auckland. Attempts are being made to redress the balance by bringing heavy industry back to the south, but the north continues to grow at a faster rate.

Perhaps the scales will turn naturally wnen residents of the more crowded northern cities look south and see what has been left behind. Wide-open spaces, frontiers and unspoiled places are still there for all who seek them. There are fine bathing beaches and fruitful fishing grounds. Rich market gardens, orchards and vineyards have their places in the south, and forests, wild rivers, waterfalls and hot pools can be found there, too.

The bigger cities have jealously hung on to trees, gardens and waterways. Wherever possible these have been kept carefully maintained so there is always a retreat from the oppressiveness of the concrete jungle.

But, above all, the mountains reign supreme. Less than 25 per cent of New Zealand's surface is under 200 metres above sea level, and the South Island is more mountainous than the North. Coupled with mountains are hauntingly beautiful glacial lakes, some of which are more than 300 metres deep.

On the east coast there are wide, dry plains, across which braided rivers bring water from melted snow. To the west of the Southern Alps are rain forests, and on both sides of the mountains huge glaciers creak and groan in their frozen courses.

In Central Otago the autumn leaves each year turn a rich, burning gold, and everywhere are reminders of those who came in quest of metal of a similar hue. In the south-western corner, among the fiords and mountains that make up the Fiordland National Park, a sense of mystery and timelessness prevails.

New Zealand and its South Island are still young, vital and partly formed. For settlers there are still lands to claim; for travellers there are sights that retain an undiscovered air; and for everyone there are experiences to be had that attest to the uniqueness of Te Waka a Maui — the canoe of Maui.

1. A coastal scene near Punakaiki.

2. A Mount Gerald ski tour. Skiers can leave from and return to the ski area by plane.

2

1. Sometimes it is almost a millpond, but every so often the Roaring Forties help Cook Strait live up to its reputation as one of the roughest stretches of water in the world. The twenty-kilometre-wide gap between New Zealand's North and South Islands takes its name from the 18th-Century British explorer, Captain James Cook, who first charted its waters and experienced its unpredictable moods. Stocky, specially designed ferries, such as this one seen near the entrance to the South Island's Tory Channel, take about three hours and twenty minutes to make the crossing from Wellington in the North Island to Picton in the South.

2. 3. Tory Channel lies between Arapawa Island and the eastern finger of Queen Charlotte Sound

4

3

on the breathtaking ferry course through sheltered waters to Picton, the southern terminal. Early last century seamen in this area were always on the lookout for whales — a pursuit which lasted until 1964 when the whaling station at Whekenui Bay was closed. The channel is named after a survey vessel which sailed through on its way to Wellington in 1839.

4. The hulk of the *Edwin Fox* provides a lonely reminder of the past, while far across the glassy surface of Queen Charlotte Sound a ferry slides by. On 31 January 1770 Captain Cook went ashore from his barque *Endeavour* in Ship Cove, claimed the South Island for King George III and named the sound after the monarch's consort, Queen Charlotte Sophie.

2

3

1. Picton may be journey's end for the ferry crossing from Wellington, but each year it is the starting point for thousands of South Island holidays. It's also the beginning of the southern half of the main-trunk railway line and State Highway 1, which run down the eastern coast of the island. Snuggled deep in the folds of Queen Charlotte Sound, Picton offers the charms of serenity, magnificent fishing, spectacular scenery, delightful bush walks and a sense of history just made.

2. A timeless view of Queen Charlotte Sound from Grove Road. Perhaps it looked like this two centuries ago when a young botanist aboard the *Endeavour*, whose later knighthood made him Sir Joseph Banks, wrote in his journal: "I was awakened by the singing of the birds ashore, from whence we are distant not a quarter of a mile. They seemed to strain their throats with emulation, and made, perhaps, the most melodious wild music I have ever heard, almost emulating small bells, but with the most tunable silver sound imaginable."

3. Tuataras caused great consternation among naturalists in Europe last century when it was discovered they were not lizards, but living links with the reptiles that roamed the earth in the dim past. They are found mostly on New Zealand's offshore islands, and some about sixty centimetres long have been estimated to be 150 years old. (Some estimates have ranged up to 300 years because little is known about these remarkable reptiles.)

1

2

1. For those who want to bottle up part of their holiday and take it home to savour, the vineyards at Renwick are a recommended stopover. Renwick, situated about thirteen kilometres from the township of Blenheim in central Marlborough, has long been a market-gardening area. Now it is winning renown with grapes that produce wine to tickle the most discerning palates.

2. Best Nelson hops ripening in the sun.

3. Maitai Valley from Observation Point. Who would think that in this beautiful river valley anything as ghastly as ambush and murder could occur? But in 1866, on the Maungatapu walking track which passes through the area, a gang of highwaymen robbed and murdered five travellers. Nelson is only twelve kilometres away from the Maitai Valley, which offers views such as this from Observation Point.

1. With the tower of Nelson Cathedral rising in the background, sightseers and shoppers take time out for afternoon tea at a roadside café. Nelson is the centre of a rich market-gardening area and enjoys one of the highest annual sunshine counts in New Zealand. It is the home port of a busy fishing fleet and a popular holiday and retirement centre.

2. Beside the fruits of the soil, Nelson is becoming famous for its craft products. Sculptor Karl de Smit is one of a lively group of potters, artists and craftspeople who find the atmosphere of the district does wonders for their work.

3. Suburbia, one hundred years ago. Part of pioneer Nelson is preserved in this row of practical wooden houses right on the street front.

4. In West Germany, Britain and other Common Market countries — not to mention the Middle East — the arrival of a shipment of New Zealand apples is delicious news. The odds are they come from Nelson, because with Hawke's Bay in the North Island the district competes for the title of Big Apple in the industry. Between them the two districts' export earnings are well in excess of $100 million per year.

3

4

1. Four boys, two bats and a ball add up to a test match, schoolboy-style in the farming district of Moutere, to the west of Nelson in Tasman Bay.

2. 3. Around the South Island coast there are numerous bays and inlets which make ideal places for getting away from it all. Mapua Inlet doesn't appear on many maps, but it fits into this category nicely. The Monarch butterfly, along with the shags, herons and a solitary gull are only some of the many species found in this quiet area.

4. A view of the wide expanse of Tasman Bay from Ruby Bay, which lies almost midway between Nelson and Motueka.

3

1

2

3

4

1. 2. The Kaiteriteri Beach is a popular resort area near Motueka, on the western shores of Tasman Bay. It was visited in October 1841 by Captain Arthur Wakefield, the New Zealand Company's agent for the Nelson settlement. He inspected Kaiteriteri as a possible site for Nelson township, but eventually passed it over. Nevertheless, a memorial to Captain Wakefield and the Riwaka pioneers tells of the little bay's brush with fame.

3. Adrift in a river of sparkling glass, a power-boat explores the Falls River Inlet on the western shores of Tasman Bay. But although the scene looks peaceful enough, the river earns its name by dropping more than 1,000 metres in just ten kilometres.

4. A picturesque anchorage at Torrent Bay, on the north-western shore of Tasman Bay.

1. The Cobb Valley carves its way down mountains between the Peel and Lockett Ranges. Its path is marked by the Cobb River, which first flows through the reservoir of a hydro dam and then plunges to a meeting with the Takaka River and the ocean mid-way around the curve of Golden Bay at the north-western tip of the South Island. It is beautiful, rugged bush country.

2. The nature of the scenery in Golden Bay is very similar to that of the Cobb Valley, as this view from the coast road shows. The Dutch explorer Abel Tasman previously named this area Murderers' Bay in 1642 when four of his crew were killed by Maoris. D'Urville, another explorer, called it Massacre Bay, a name kept until 1842 when the discovery of coal at Takaka put Coal Bay on the map. That name disappeared in 1857 when hunters found gold in the Aorere River, resulting in yet another new name — however, this one seems destined to last.

3. A breakwater reaches out to sea at Pohara Beach, a popular holiday area in Golden Bay, nine kilometres north-east of the township of Takaka. In the distance is the Golden Bay cement works.

2

3

1. 2. Captain James Cook named
this area Farewell Spit because it
was the last part of New Zealand
he saw as he set sail for Great
Britain — and it has been the last
piece of land seen from many a
ship that has gone aground there.
Visitors can drive down the
twenty-four-kilometre-long spit at
the north-western finger of the
South Island. A lighthouse marks
journey's end, and there's the
added attraction of a refuge for
tiny godwits which rest there in
preparation for flights half-way
around the world to Siberia.

3

3.The Takaka River saw its own brief period of gold fever in the 1850s, but now enjoys a quieter life as a tourist attraction. The region is rich in mineral deposits of various kinds and has a reputation as Marble Mountain Country, thanks to a rich seam of hard crystalline limestone.

4. Rotoiti means "small lake" in Maori, but these canoeists are enjoying one of a large range of activities available on or around this glacial lake. Boating, hiking, picnicking, swimming, hunting and skiing are all enjoyed in this part of the Nelson Lakes National Park.

4

1

2

1, 2. Once the rocky Kaikoura coastline was dotted with numerous Maori pa. Later, keen-eyed whalers waited there for their quarry to pass by. Captain Cook called the peninsula "Lookers On" after a group of Maoris in four double canoes paddled out to look at the *Endeavour*, but refused to come alongside. The peninsula itself is about 180 kilometres north of Christchurch and has a seal colony and reefs that have been designated a wildlife refuge.

3. Enjoying the wide-open spaces at Hanmer in North Canterbury. The region is best known for the Hanmer Springs spa and health resort, which has a world-wide reputation.

2

3

1. The braided pattern of many of the rivers draining the Canterbury Plains is evident in this view of the Waiau River from the Hanmer Bridge. There are five rivers of the same name in New Zealand, but this one is said in Maori legend to have once been a young girl who lived in the Spenser Mountains with her lover, Waiau-toa (the Clarence River). When the rivers are flushed with the spring thaw, the separated lovers are said to be weeping.

2. Ever since their discovery in 1859, the Hanmer Springs, with their soft and soothing waters, have drawn people seeking treatment and relaxation. Farming,

forestry, tourism, and skiing at nearby Amuri have ensured the region's prosperity.

3. Trees at Hamner on a frosty morning.

4. The 150-kilometre-long Waimakariri River rises in the glaciers of the Southern Alps, breaks free of the rocks and crags and then sprawls its way across the Canterbury Plains to the sea. Wreathed in winter mists, it leaves no doubt that its name was well chosen! Waimakariri means "cold water".

4

1. The snow-capped Southern Alps provide the frosting on the horizon in this view of Christchurch city. Sometimes the climate of the alps reaches out to the city and helps create the greatest range of temperatures of any of the main centres. The mean daily minimum in winter (July) is 1°C and the mean summer daily maximum (January) is 22°C. However, gusty föhn winds descending from the alps can send temperatures soaring to over 35°C in summer.

2. Christchurch, the largest city in the South Island, derives much of its distinctive English atmosphere from the River Avon which flows through Hagley Park en route to the sea. However, the name has Scottish rather than English origins. The original sketch map of the settlement shows it as "the River Shakespeare", but it was later renamed after a stream near Riccarton, Kilmarnock, County Ayrshire, in south-west Scotland.

3. Christchurch had its beginnings in an orderly reconstruction of the way of life many of its settlers had left behind. There are constant reminders of "The Old Country" in many of its buildings and place names. The houses in Durham Street are such a reminder and are becoming much sought after.

4. The Chamber of Commerce building is another with a familiar look about it. Peering over its brick shoulders is a relative newcomer, Noah's Hotel.

5. Like a brace of misty lollipops, the twin sprays of the Ferrier Fountain give a softening touch to the walls of the Christchurch Town Hall. The complex, opened in 1972, includes the James Hay theatre, which seats more than 1,000 people; an oval-shaped auditorium seating another 2,660; the Limes Room for banquets, balls and other functions; a restaurant and public concourse areas. The Town Hall was the venue for some of the activities of the Commonwealth Games in 1974.

2

3

4

1. As early as 1864 the people of Christchurch set about building their cathedral, which now dominates Cathedral Square in the centre of the city. However, the construction was beset with problems due to difficult economic times. The nave was not ready for use until 1881, and the transepts and chancel were opened in 1904. The Gothic-style building is said to have been modelled on that of Caen Cathedral in Normandy.

2. Lancaster Park is known to rugby and cricket fans the world over as an arena where history has been made and sporting heroics have inspired legends. However, it has seen much more than cricket and rugby. Olympic runner Peter Snell set two world records there, and soccer, rugby league, tennis and even swimming have had their great moments on or near the hallowed turf.

3. The Roman Catholic Basilica, the Cathedral of the Blessed Sacrament, is holy ground of a more traditional kind. This imposing Roman Renaissance-style building in Barbadoes Street was designed by Francis William Petre.

4. Inside it is even more impressive with its massive dome above the altar and an air of space and graciousness.

1

2

3

4

1, 2. The gardens and parks of Christchurch are a constant delight, but chief among them is Hagley Park, which would be the envy of much larger cities around the world. The 200-hectare park was named after the family estate of the Fourth Baron Lyttelton, who was chairman of the Canterbury Association in 1849. It includes numerous sports grounds, the city's Botanic Gardens, a golf course and several specialty gardens. On the eastern side of the park is the Canterbury Museum, which houses one of the finest ornithological collections in the Southern Hemisphere, and many fine pioneer displays.

3. Looking at Christchurch today it is difficult to believe it ever passed through a rough-and-ready pioneer stage. Everything seems too well planned and orderly, right down to the neatly-clipped grass for the polo ponies. The Town Hall underlines the Christchurch citizen's love of culture, but sport has also been strong from the early days — especially those activities favoured by the English.

4. "The Golden Half-Mile" at Brighton is one of the busiest shopping centres in Christchurch.

1. A searchlight mirror provides
a lot of fun in its second life at the
Ferrymead Historic Park,
Christchurch.

2. Lyttelton Harbour — a quiet
anchorage for yachts and other
pleasure craft.

1. This immigrant, who received VIP treatment all the way to Orana Park at Christchurch, gets plenty of callers each day and treats them with regal indifference.

2. Sumner Beach, a pleasant retreat just 11 kilometres from the centre of Christchurch.

3. Looking towards Little River from Lake Forsyth, Banks Peninsula.

4. Akaroa Harbour.

3

4

1. A baton change for relay racers on Summit Road in the Port Hills, Christchurch, as they pound their way towards Akaroa.

2. The settlement of Akaroa, nestling in its sheltered harbour, was once a base for whalers and could easily have become another French territory in the South Pacific. In 1838, Jean Langlois, the master of the *Cachalot*, negotiated with the local Maori people to buy the whole of Banks Peninsula. He made a downpayment and returned to France to arrange a company of settlers. Before they arrived, the Treaty of Waitangi had been signed, making New Zealand a colony of Great Britain.

1

2

1. Governor Hobson assured the French that their property would be respected, but to make his position clear he sent Captain Owen Stanley in HMS *Britomart* to hoist the British flag at Akaroa. A monument at Green's Point marks the site where this was accomplished on 11 August 1840. Another reminder is one of the *Britomart's* guns mounted in a park setting overlooking the harbour.

2. Dinghies provide a splash of colour on Akaroa's waterfront.

3

3. An old try-pot, providing mute testimony to the endeavours of whalers in the Akaroa area.

4. Langlois-Enteveneaux House, with French street signs outside, firmly establishes the French presence in its role as a museum. Rue Lavaud honours the captain of *L'Aube*, a French naval corvette, which accompanied Langlois' party of settlers aboard the *Comte de Paris*.

4

1. Part rogue, part robber, part clown — the kea will remove anything from a camp site that isn't tied down, and he will entertain you with his antics as he does so. The hooked beak reveals that he is a bird of prey, and some high country farmers would call him killer as well, blaming him for vicious attacks on sheep. That apart, the kea is sure to charm visitors to the South Island's high-country regions.

2. When naturalist Sir Joseph Banks wrote in 1770 of waking to the sound of beautiful bird song like small silver bells, one of the culprits probably was what is now called a bellbird. To ornithologists this forest mimic is known as *Anthornis melanura*, and the Maori people have assigned the more melodic name of korimako.

3. A precarious-looking road cuts through the formidable Otira Gorge, connecting Westland and Canterbury. In pioneer times, stage coaches rattled back and forth regularly, keeping open this important route for passengers and commerce. The eight-and-a-half-kilometre Otira railway tunnel brought new ease to the journey.

4. Magnificent native bush dominates the scenery on the Heaphy Track, which links Bainham in Golden Bay and Karamea on the West Coast. Trampers usually allow four to six days for the journey.

1. Even the highway over Karamea Bluff is lined with bush.

2. When the first batch of assisted immigrants sponsored by the Nelson Provincial Government moved into the Karamea area in 1874, they had high hopes for a prosperous future. However, nature treated them unkindly and many walked off their properties, discouraged by the bush and clay soil. Some who battled on gave up after the severe Murchison earthquake wrecked the district's port and roads in 1929. The descendants of those who stayed now reap the benefits.

3. Often the West Coast highway swings close to the surf and hugs the shoreline around abrupt headlands, such as these near Punakaiki, a farming district forty-two kilometres north of Greymouth.

4. In a different mood, much of the West Coast is still as wild and mysterious as it was in the times of New Zealand's early explorers.

3

4

1

2

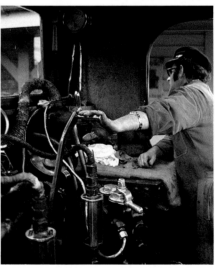

3

3. On the site of an old goldfield, enterprising West Coasters have erected Shantytown, a life-sized replica of a New Zealand frontier town. There visitors can walk the streets of a mining town of the 1880s, browse through 19th-Century shops or ride behind the ancient locomotive, Kaitangata, to a gold claim where they can try their luck. Shantytown is located at Rutherglen, ten kilometres south of Greymouth.

4. The fishing fleet at Greymouth, the West Coast's chief commercial centre.

1. 2. Certainly not like mother used to make, the Punakaiki pancakes are actually fluted limestone rocks, carved by the rushing surf and fierce blowholes in the area. The display is accompanied by awesome rumblings and boomings as the sea continues its sculpting. The Pancake Rocks are situated to the south of Punakaiki township, near the mouth of the Punakaiki River.

5. Lake Kaniere from the eastern shore. The lake, situated approx. 18 km from Hokitika, frequently provides visitors with superb reflections. It is a favourite for waterskiers, swimmers, picnickers and fishermen.

4

5

1

1. The Lake Kaniere area in a
misty mood.

2. The Heaphy Track, regarded
as one of the country's most
spectacular walks, bursts out
to a magnificent sweep of
isolated, sandy coastline
at Scotts Beach.

2

presented to King George V as a Coronation gift and was melted down for a tea service.

3. Don't expect to have the road to yourself on the West Coast — the livestock are often going places, too. This motor-cycle sheep-herder is plying his trade near Harihari in South Westland.

1, 2. Who knows how much more gold the Westland bush conceals? "Not much", old-timers might say as they watch travellers motor by on the sealed highway near Ross. But it doesn't stop them talking about "the Honourable Roddy", a 2,807-gram nugget found near the township in 1903 by John Scott and Arthur Sharp. It was later

1

2

1. Although Lake Matheson was an afterthought of the Fox Glacier, it is high on the list of priorities for tourists, particularly photographers who make much of the beautiful reflections of distant mountains. As the glacier retreated, it left an isolated pocket of ice behind in a depression. When the ice melted, Lake Matheson was born.

2. Most people go to the beach to fish or swim, but in April 1866 James Edwin Gillespie found gold here. The Westland beach that now bears his name looks less than inviting here, but it soon supported a busy mining operation, signs of which can still be seen.

3. The massive Southern Alps have produced some of the biggest glaciers outside the Himalayas and polar regions. However, here the Fox Glacier seems small far in the distance, its blue-white expanse blending with the early-morning sky and clouds.

3. Snowfields surrounding the fifteen-kilometre-long Fox Glacier help to conceal treacherous crevasses as it makes its majestic descent from just over 2,700 metres above sea level to only 245 metres. The Fox Glacier township at the edge of the river flat below the glacier is a popular and well-equipped tourist resort. The glacier had royal beginnings, first being named after Prince Alfred (Queen Victoria's second son) and then "Prince Albert" after the Queen's consort. The final "Fox" honours Sir William Fox, who was four times Prime Minister of New Zealand.

4. Fishing boats shelter in the calm waters of Jackson Bay, a Westland fishing port south of the Haast River.

5. A glimpse of Lake Moeraki which lies on the coast north of Haast.

1. Keeping a wary eye on passers-by along a bush path is a wood pigeon, or Kereru. Once a popular gamebird of the Maori, it is now protected.

2. The Minehaha bush walk is one of several interesting hikes that may be made in the glacier area.

3

4

5

1. In all of the Southern Alps Mount Tasman is second only to Mount Cook. Named after the Dutch explorer who was the first of the European wanderers to discover New Zealand, Mount Tasman reaches 3,498 metres skyward, offering a constant challenge to climbers.

2. Skiers come from all over the world to enjoy the snow at Mount Hutt, which rises from the Canterbury Plains 108 kilometres south-west of Christchurch. Part of its popularity is due to its relative closeness to the city of Christchurch, and part to the long skiing season, which extends from May till October.

3. From its pastures New Zealand earns 75 per cent of its overseas income. Sheep outnumber humans more than twenty to one, and New Zealand ranks in the top three trading nations for most agricultural products. This field of clover is near Prebbleton, a township thirteen kilometres south-west of Christchurch.

1. Evening begins to cast its shadows over farmland at Fairlie in South Canterbury. The district was given its name by early settlers because of its resemblance to Fairlie in Strathclyde, Western Scotland.

2. Bob Anderson discusses some of the features of the Rodgers engine he restored after it was recovered from the Oreti River in Southland. The engine hauled the first Christchurch-Dunedin express and, as the original "Kingston Flyer", earned fame in the Queenstown area. A love for things of the past is particularly strong in the south.

3

4

3. Few churches in New Zealand are as much photographed or beloved to photographers as the Church of the Good Shepherd at Lake Tekapo in South Canterbury. The lake covers eighty-three square kilometres and is tucked into the eastern fringe of the Southern Alps. The simple stone church was built in 1935 as a memorial to the pioneer runholders of the Mackenzie Country, as the high-country grasslands are known.

4. There is no need for stained glass with windows like these. This view of the lake is from inside the church, looking out over the altar.

1

2

1. At the best of times the water of the lake is rather cold for swimming, but in winter Lake Tekapo's garb echoes its glacial birth.

2. Lake Pukaki, a near neighbour of Tekapo. The cool, blue water and its icy surrounds impersonate the mountains and sky. The reflection is so crisp you may have to mark the tops and bottoms of your photographs to avoid displaying them upside down by mistake. Like Tekapo, Lake Pukaki is of glacial origin and contributes water to hydro-electric power schemes.

3. Mount Cook towers above the placid waters of Lake Pukaki.

4. Mount Cook's Maori name is Aorangi, or cloud piercer, and it dominates the tourist resort area at its base in the Mount Cook National Park. The scenic beauty and range of alpine activities bring tourists and climbers from all over the world.

3

4

1. Mount Cook, with dawn etching out the three peaks covered by climbers attempting the grand traverse.

3. Ski-plane flights around the Mount Cook region cram days of sight-seeing into a few minutes. The sensation is one of being surrounded by expanse after expanse of snow-covered peaks and valleys. For a climax the plane may land on a snowfield high in the mountains. Mount Cook in the background is, at 3,764 metres, New Zealand's highest peak.

2. The Mount Cook lily (*Ranunculus lyalli*), actually a mountain buttercup, is probably the most familiar of New Zealand alpine flowers. For those who rarely visit Mount Cook, the lily is recognised on aircraft and buses as the symbol of Mount Cook Airlines.

4. The Hermitage, a famous tourist hotel in Mount Cook Village, has been the starting point for many expeditions. Sir Edmund Hillary, the New Zealander who became the first man to climb Mount Everest, did much of his early mountaineering in the Mount Cook National Park.

5. A solitary alpine hut perched on the Tasman Saddle.

4

5

1

2

3

1. Easy ski slopes lead down to the gigantic and other-worldly Tasman Glacier — a twenty-nine kilometre staircase which descends to the valley floor. It is the largest glacier in New Zealand and one of the longest found in a temperate zone. The glacier and the river that emerges from beneath it were named after the explorer Abel Tasman.

2. Tinged with pink early-morning light, Mount Sefton (3,157 metres) greets a new day from this vantage point overlooking the confluence of the Hooker and Mueller Glaciers near Mount Cook.

3. The Ohau Range to the west of Lake Ohau forms the boundary between the Mackenzie County in South Canterbury and the Waitaki County in Central Otago. A skifield for advanced and intermediate skiers looks out over the lake below.

4, 5. The Lindis Pass in summer, and dressed for winter. An Otago surveyor, John Turnbull Thompson, discovered the pass in December 1857 and named it after the holy island of Lindisfarne off the coast of Northumberland, in north-east England. A monument on the pass marks the point where red deer were released in 1871. In the absence of natural predators, the deer flourished.

4

5

1

1. The spreading green of a lucerne farm at Luggate, near Wanaka. In the gold-rush era, farmlands further north produced wheat which was milled at Luggate and found a ready market with the miners.

2. When miners and settlers first moved into Central Otago they used the ever-present stone as a building material. Often the shacks, outbuildings and walls they constructed so cleverly were erected without the use of mortar. Examples of such work can be found at Bendigo on the eastern banks of the Clutha River.

2

3. Sheep graze on the fertile
Clutha Valley river flats near Tarras
in Central Otago.

3

1

2

3

1. The annual blossom festival each September at Alexandra, Central Otago, is a time of thanksgiving and goodwill for this rich farming land near the junction of the Clutha and Manuherikia Rivers. People come for many miles to see the parade and join in the festivities.

2. A shepherd, aided by his dogs, moves sheep between paddocks lined by lupins.

3 .4. Everywhere at St Bathans are signs of the miners who came, struggled for gold and left when the supply dwindled. One of the few buildings on the old main street still in good repair is the Vulcan Hotel, which dates from 1869. Blue Lake, a crater 800 metres long and more than fifty metres deep, is the result of a massive excavation by miners, and is now filled with water. In winter it freezes over to provide an excellent rink for skating and curling.

4

1. It is easy to assume Waimate was always like this, but the township had its beginning only last century in a meeting between two men in 1854. A settler, Michael Studholme, and a Maori chief, Te Huruhuru, negotiated the sale of the land somewhere near the end of this avenue.

2. The nature of the land changes from mountains to the plains of South Canterbury near Waimate, with stooks of hay in the foreground and the shadows of the Hunter Hills beyond.

3

3. The Roman Catholic basilica in Timaru dates back to 1910 and shows that the people of the day enjoyed the sense of permanence created by imposing buildings in brick and stone. Timaru, the centre of South Canterbury, celebrated its centenary in 1968.

4. Approaching squall near Oamaru.

4

3

4

1. There is a richness about the land and its colours that marks the south as a special place. Something of this quality shows here in this view from the Haast Highway near Makaroa.

2. Lovely enough to be the subject of an oil painting, Lake Wanaka parallels Lake Hawea on the other side of the road leading to the Haast. Although it is forty-five kilometres long, Lake Wanaka is only six kilometres across at its widest point — a clue to its glacial origin. While elsewhere in Otago others were looking for gold, settlers around Wanaka established huge sheep stations and made their fortunes from wool and lamb.

3. In places Lake Wanaka is more than 300 metres deep, but most people see only the limpid surface before brilliant surrounding foliage steals their eyes away.

4. Delicate fronds of toe-toe curve with the wind against a backdrop of 3,027-metre Mount Aspiring near the southern reaches of the Southern Alps. Mount Aspiring, which in some respects has been likened to the Matterhorn in Switzerland, forms a natural boundary between the lakes of Central Otago and the rain forests of Westland.

1. Miners came and went, but the farmers stayed. That's the story of the beautiful Cardrona Valley, named by a Scotsman, Robert Wilkin, the first runholder in the Wanaka region. Cardrona lies on the eyecatching route between Lake Wanaka and Queenstown — the highest highway in New Zealand.

2. During the height of the gold rush, Cardrona's population reached 5,000, and saloons such as the historic Cardrona Hotel did a roaring trade. Sometimes there was a bit too much roaring, and the trade was in punches. Storekeepers and publicans often used their own security forces to preserve the peace.

3. This pioneer cottage is in a street of cottages in the centre of Arrowtown, on the banks of the Arrow River. These days the most obvious gold gleams from the branches of the trees that arch over the main street. A must for visitors, whether in search of gold or history, is a visit to the Lake County Museum where the region's past is most commendably preserved.

4. When beautiful Lake Hayes was named after its discoverer, an Australian stockman named Donald Hay, his name was misspelled. What is more, when Hay arrived in Dunedin to apply for lakeside pasture land, he found the news had preceded him and a claim had been lodged by an employee of the Lands and Survey office. Lake Hayes is situated between Queenstown and Arrowtown, and is renowned for its excellent fishing.

1

2

3

1

2

1. In 1863 a public meeting at a small settlement on the shores of Lake Wakatipu decided the township site was fit for a queen — so they called it Queenstown. Now it is one of the major tourist areas of New Zealand, and among its attractions features a cableway to a restaurant at the top of Bob's Peak. The awesome view of the lake and surrounding countryside is guaranteed to sharpen any appetite for more of what the region has to offer.

2. Paddles ply the water in unison as canoeists head out across the Frankton arm of Lake Wakatipu. The mountain range in the background was named The Remarkables by a pioneer Otago surveyor, Alexander Garvie, in 1857. Covering some 291 square kilometres, Wakatipu is the longest lake in the South Island and the third largest in New Zealand. Every five minutes or so the lake level rises and falls as much as twelve centimetres, a phenomenon scientists say is due to either wind or variations in atmospheric pressure. Maori legend has it that the pulsing is caused by the heart of a deposed giant.

3 — 5. In winter The Remarkables range is covered in snow; in summer it stands as gaunt, baked stone, with remarkable presence. The highest point is Double Cone, which reaches 2,343 metres. The extremely rugged nature of The Remarkables gives the range a grandeur missing from other more gently moulded mountains.

6. Waterlilies, Queenstown.

3 — 5

6

1. Hundreds of prospectors swarmed to the Arrow River in the 1860s after a share of the significant amounts of gold that were taken out of what is sometimes regarded as little more than a mountain stream. Fossickers and holiday-makers still try their luck with pan and shovel, and are often rewarded with traces of colour.

2. Hell's Gate is an appropriate introduction to what lies beyond in Skippers Canyon. The "gate" is one of many awesome features of the thirty-two kilometres of scary road, track and cliffside ledge that have been chipped through this gorge near Queenstown. While not for the faint-hearted, it has provided a popular day-trip for tourists.

3. "Skippers", as it is often called, is said to have been named after a ship's captain whose vessel was wrecked near the Otago Heads. The Skipper, as he was known to all, made his way to Queenstown and discovered gold in the gorge in the 1860s. A dredge worked these waters as recently as the 1930s.

4. Winding up the Shotover River at seventy kilometres/hour in a jetboat is the highlight of many southern holidays. In spite of the speed of the boats — a New Zealand invention — and the rugged nature of the surroundings, the thrills are as safe as a fairground ride.

1. The Shotover River carves its way through hills and rocks until it reaches the Kawarau River about two kilometres to the east of Frankton, which is in turn only ten kilometres east of Queenstown. Jetboat rides up the river offer a fast and exciting way to see the numerous reminders of the river's golden past. One of the best-known stories of the Shotover tells how two shearers made the first gold strike on 15 November 1862, taking 200 ounces of gold from the river in a week.

2. The bus trip up the canyon stops at the Skippers Bridge, a one hundred-metre suspension bridge passing over the Shotover River to the site of the abandoned Skippers township. A few of the original residents are still there — in a pioneer cemetery. However, there is a homestead for the runholder and his family.

3. One hundred years ago, the Queenstown area was home for a cosmopolitan mixture of races and creeds lured by the search for gold. Today the mixture is still there, but the crowds are tourists or skiers. Rex and Trevor Woodbury didn't want to lose the flavour of the old days completely, so they built Golden Terrace mining town, as a tribute to the past. The buildings are filled with authentic bric-a-brac of bygone years, which recreate the feeling of the gold mining times.

2

3

When summer goes,
Queenstown barely misses a beat.
Winter tourists arrive in their
thousands to pit themselves
against the ski slopes of Coronet
Peak. The facilities are excellent
and include instruction for
beginners. Ski lifts and tows
provide easy access to the
best snow and make it possible
for skiers to spend all day on
slopes of their choice. Although
they had been used by local skiers
since the early days of this
century, the fields were first
developed by members of the
Wigley family after they flew over
the area and realised its potential.

1. With her smart, red funnel towering high above boarding passengers, the S.S. *Earnslaw* prepares to make yet another cruise on Lake Wakatipu. She made her debut soon after the Railways Department purchased all privately owned service shipping on the lake in 1911, and proceeded to win hearts by the thousand. Fifty years later the *Earnslaw* was a legend, but roads and road transport had improved enormously and provided too much competition for the ferry. In 1968, the Railways Department decided to scrap her.

2. Luckily, the public outcry that greeted the announcement forced a change of heart and the *Earnslaw*, now under private ownership, still carries passengers across the lake. There are faster ways to travel, but none would dispute that the *Earnslaw* is something special.

3. The Kawarau River makes its exit from Lake Wakatipu on the Frankton Arm.

1. Farming, which began in Arrowtown when the gold started to run out, is still thriving.

2. You are welcome to come hunting — with cameras, not guns — at Deer Park Heights near Queenstown. Here, in their natural habitat, it is possible to see deer, chamois, thar and other alpine animals at their best.

3. The head of Lake Wakatipu and Mount Earnslaw as seen from Glenorchy, the starting point for tramping trips and climbing trips in the Rees Valley and neighbouring mountains.

4. Trampers arrive at the start of the forty-kilometre Routeburn Track. The three-to-four-day hike links the Queenstown region with Fiordland. Trampers traverse the southern reaches of the Southern Alps, passing through Mount Aspiring and Fiordland National Parks.

5. In pre-European times and perhaps as recently as 1852, the Maori people used the Routeburn track to get access to West Coast greenstone and preserve trading links with villages in South Westland. Today a sense of adventure prevails for all who make the trek through these valleys, mountains and forest paths.

6. A silver fern is New Zealand's national emblem. This, and ferns of many other types, may be seen all along the track.

4

5

6

1

2

1. The Moeraki Boulders have puzzled people for generations — they lie upon the east-coast beach like giant marbles abandoned by giant children. A Maori legend says they are the petrified remains of seed kumara and cargo washed ashore from a capsized canoe; however, the scientific explanation is more prosaic. They are septarian concretions formed millions of years ago by the accumulation of limestone salts on the sea floor. They can be seen between the fishing village of Moeraki and the township of Hampden.

2,3. The tidal flats of Otago Peninsula are teeming with life, ranging from tiny sea creatures to the majestic Royal Albatross with a wing-span of up to three-and-a-half metres. Penguins, gulls and wading birds fuss around the crags, and shags bob about in search of prey. The Royal Albatross colony on Taiaroa Head falls within the boundary of Dunedin City, and is the only one in the world so close to civilisation.

4. Looking north from Waitati towards Blueskin Bay.

1

2

fascinating collection of relics from whaling and mining days, early paintings and photographs, diaries, furniture and farm equipment. The displays are rated among the best in the Southern Hemisphere.

5. Dunedin's Law Courts present a facade of elaborate stonework.

1. The gold rush helped make Dunedin the business centre of New Zealand in the late 19th Century. This is still demonstrated today by the stately homes of merchant princes of yester-year — among them two castles. The city now takes pride in its many fine gardens and homes, some of which are open to the public.

2. George Street to the north and Princes Street to the south are the main thoroughfares in Dunedin City. They meet at the Octagon from where all commercial life radiates under the watchful eyes of a statue of Robbie Burns. Many of the churches cluster around the Octagon as well.

3. Dunedin was founded in 1848 as a Free Church of Scotland settlement, and the Presbyterian influence has always been strong in spite of the pot-pourri of races originally attracted by the search for gold. The present First Church was built in a Gothic Revivalist style and dates from 1873. Local hard, grey stone was used for the base and walls, while the decorative touches were wrought from some of the finest Oamaru stone ever quarried.

4. This cable car has its last resting place in the Otago Early Settlers Association Museum and Portrait Gallery in Dunedin. It is in good company among a

1. Despite its beauty and size,
Lake Te Anau works for a living.
Some of the water from this, the
largest South Island lake,
discharges into the Waiau River
which flows into Lake Manapouri
and helps feed the massive

Manapouri hydro-electric project.
There are enough activities
available on and around the lake
to keep visitors busy for many
days, among them the
world-famous Milford Track walk,
which begins at Glade House.

2. The Eglinton valley provides
entry to Fiordland National Park
from Te Anau, offering
incomparable scenery along the
way.

1

2

3

1. Perhaps the most easily-recognised feature of Milford Sound is Mitre Peak, which spears upward for 1,692 metres to become one of the world's highest mountains rising directly from the sea. Its name was bestowed upon it because of the peak's resemblance to a bishop's headgear.

2. An "Islander" lands at the Milford Sound airstrip, which provides the speediest link with the outside world. Sometimes this is the only link as storms can cut off the highway leading to the Milford resort area.

3. Sudden weather changes are common in Milford Sound and along the Milford Track, "the finest walk in the world". Here the forbidding outline of Mitre Peak is a reminder to climbers that it is not to be taken lightly.

1. When mountains are coupled with a steady rainfall, the result is high waterfalls, with which Milford Sound abounds. The Bowen Falls drop in two stages for 160 metres en route from the Bowen River to Milford Sound. They are named after a 19th-Century governor of New Zealand, Sir George Ferguson Bowen.

2. "As idle as a painted ship upon a painted ocean ..." Usually anything but idle, this yacht called in at Milford Sound from Auckland during a circumnavigation of New Zealand.

3. The northern side of Milford Sound is dominated by Mount Pembroke (2,045 metres), which looms above the Palisades ridge. It is thought that Mount Pembroke was given its name by John Grono, a pioneer Welsh sealer, in memory of the town of Pembroke in his home country.

2

3

1. Large cruise ships often enter Milford Sound and anchor at Harrison Cove. Although its attractiveness would justify a stopover, the cove is the only suitable anchorage in the area.

2. Rudyard Kipling called Milford Sound the eighth wonder of the world. The Nobel Prize-winning author chose his words carefully, and few would argue that the sound, a true Norwegian-style fiord, does not deserve such praise. The approach from the sea shows the sheerness of its glacially-carved walls, and the inner reaches are deeper than the entrance. The entrance-way is an invitation to adventurers everywhere.

3. The Chasm, where the roaring Cleddau River has carved its way through solid rock near the road to Milford.

1. For many years the
Sutherland Falls were thought to
be the highest in the world. Now
they are ranked number five, but
they still rate as a heart-stopping
spectacle as they plunge in three
great leaps from Lake Quill in the
sky to the valley of the Arthur
River. They were discovered on 10
November 1880 by Scotsman
Donald Sutherland. The three
stages drop in turn 248 metres,
229 metres and 103 metres.

2. A walker on the Milford Track,
which stretches from the head of
Lake Te Anau to Milford Sound.

3. Yet another spectacle among the myriad waterfalls which seam the cliffs and mountainsides of Fiordland: this is Gate Pa Falls on the Milford Track.

4. The scenic Arthur River framed by bush.

3

4

1. A basket of wriggling, pink crays, which take on a distinctive orange hue when cooked.

2. Crayfishermen at work in the lonely waters of Fiordland. Their catch could grace tables in New Zealand, or in North America as rock lobster.

3. Milford Sound offers a bewildering array of breathtaking subjects for artists, such as this summer mountain scene.

4. In the Murchison Mountains near Te Anau, ornithologists made a startling discovery. One of New Zealand's flightless birds, the Takahe (*Notornis mantelli*) was thought to have joined the Moa in extinction, but in November 1948 a small colony was discovered. The Murchison Mountains are now a specially protected wilderness area to ensure the Takahe's survival.

5. A green parakeet, an Australian visitor that stayed to add its attractions to those of Milford Sound.

1. Coal trucks rumble through the snow from the Southland mining town of Nightcaps. The locality takes its name from that given to strange, conical hills nearby, which resemble night-time headgear. The deep south is one of the few areas of generally temperate New Zealand where snow falls outside the mountain ranges.

2. This imposing memorial to the Boer War stands in Invercargill, New Zealand's most southern city and certainly the most distant corner of the British Empire to respond to the call to arms in the South African conflict.

3. The colourful bricks and striking design of the First (Presbyterian) Church, Invercargill, have made it a landmark in the city since 1915. There are surprises inside, too, such as a sculptured wood panel of the Last Supper which was purchased in Venice by a pioneer pastor, Thomas Spencer Forsaith.

4. Raking leaves in Queens Park, an eighty-hectare reserve in the centre of Invercargill. This showplace of the city has had an interesting past, including time as a racecourse and sportsground. Now great care has been taken to develop an outstanding array of floral delights, a wildlife sanctuary, an aviary and a children's park.

5. Strollers enjoy a golden autumn avenue within the park.

4

5

Each year the nation's
gourmets cast anxious glances
south and wonder how the Bluff
oyster catch is faring. Bluff is
situated near the end of a
peninsula which reaches out into
Foveaux Strait between the South
Island and Stewart Island. The
surrounding waters abound with
fish, among which the famed Bluff
oysters hold a place of honour.

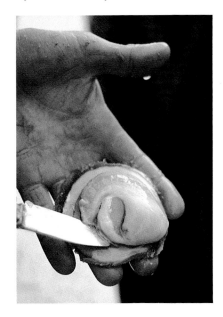

1

2

1. According to Maori legend, the North Island was a fish caught by the demi-god Maui from his canoe, the South Island. Some thirty kilometres south of the canoe is Stewart Island, said to be its anchor stone. When Captain James Cook sighted it, he wasn't sure whether he was seeing an island or a peninsula, so he cautiously named it South Cape. The principal settlement is Oban in Halfmoon Bay, where small craft abound.

2. Halfmoon Bay is where many of the bush walks and cruises to neighbouring islands begin.

3. The deeply indented coastline of Stewart Island gives it great scenic beauty.

4. Golden Bay, a cove on Paterson Inlet, a kilometre to the south-west, is also a good place for messing about in boats.

3

4

Dawn at Halfmoon Bay.